Dick Cheney

Elaine Andrews

Dick Cheney

A LIFE IN PUBLIC SERVICE

A Gateway Biography

The Millbrook Press
Brookfield, Connecticut

Cover photograph courtesy of © Liaison Agency/Ken Cedeno

Photographs courtesy of AP/Wide World Photos: pp. 6, 9, 20, 35, 40, 42;
Office of Vice President Cheney: pp. 10, 33; ClassMates.Com Yearbook Archives:
pp. 12, 13; American Heritage Center, University of Wyoming: p. 16; Casper
College Library: p. 24 (*Casper Star-Tribune* Collection); Corbis: pp. 21, 27 (©
Reuters), 30, 31 (©UPI/Bettmann), 37 (© AFP), 44 (Reuters NewMedia, Inc.)

Library of Congress Cataloging-in-Publication Data

Andrews, Elaine K.
Dick Cheney : a life in public service / Elaine Andrews.
p. cm.—(A Gateway biography)
Includes bibliographical references (p.) and index.
ISBN 0-7613-2306-6 (lib. bdg.)
1. Cheney, Richard B.—Juvenile literature. 2. Vice-Presidents—
United States—Biography—Juvenile literature.
[1. Cheney, Richard B. 2. Vice-Presidents.] I. Title. II. Series.
E840.8.C43 a54 2001   973.931—dc21
[B]   2001030285

Published by The Millbrook Press, Inc.
2 Old New Milford Road
Brookfield, Connecticut 06804
www.millbrookpress.com

CONTENTS

With their wives by their sides, Dick Cheney (left)
and George W. (right) campaigned hard during
Campaign 2000. Often supporters with a shower
of confetti greeted the candidates.

It was the morning of July 26, 2000. About 1,800 residents of Casper, Wyoming, crowded into a high-school gym. More than 2,500 other people waited outside. Everyone was excited. They were waiting to greet Dick Cheney and Texas governor George W. Bush. George W. Bush was the Republican candidate for U.S. president. Dick Cheney was the Republican candidate for vice president.

When the two men and their wives finally arrived, the people broke into cheers. The crowd waved American flags and chanted: "Bush, Cheney. Bush, Cheney. Bush, Cheney." The two men smiled and waved.

The people were especially happy to see Dick Cheney. He had grown up in Casper. Then he had gone on to a career in public service. Now he was running for the second highest office in the land. He was a hometown hero. The people of Casper could not have been prouder.

Dick Cheney spoke to the people. "It's a great pleasure

to look out over the crowd and see so many friends and people who have supported us over the years," he said. Restaurant owner Tom Kindler praised Dick Cheney: "Everyone in Casper knows him. He's an honest, down-to-earth person. . . . It gives me goose bumps to think about Cheney as vice president."

Childhood Years

THE MAN WHO WOULD BE VICE PRESIDENT of the United States was born on January 30, 1941, in Lincoln, Nebraska. He was the first of three children born to Richard and Marjorie Dickey Cheney. His parents named him Richard Bruce at birth. But early on, young Richard Bruce preferred to be called Dick. The name stuck.

Dick's father and mother had lived through the Great Depression of the 1930s. It was a time when millions of Americans had no jobs. Many lost all their money. People in Nebraska also lost their farms and ranches. Dick's parents knew what it was like to have to work hard and do without things.

Dick's father came from a small town. His family had suffered greatly during the Depression. He had to quit college to find a job.

In Lincoln, Dick's father worked for the U.S. Department of Agriculture. He advised farmers and ranchers about ways to conserve, or protect, their land. Marjorie

Cheney also worked. Dick's parents were determined that their children would have a normal, happy childhood.

Young Dick went to elementary school in Lincoln. He liked school and was a good student. He also liked sports, including baseball. He and his brother, Bobby, played on a midget baseball team. Dick always tried

Dick (far right) with his brother, Bobby (second from left), proved his athletic ability early on when he joined the midget baseball team in Lincoln.

hard to win. Perhaps Dick got his love of baseball from his mother. Marjorie Cheney had once played on a woman's championship softball team.

Dick also loved the outdoors. He enjoyed hiking and camping and especially fishing. A childhood friend remembers that even in fishing, Dick wanted to be the best: "It was, 'I caught seven fish and you only caught six.'"

As a Boy Scout, Dick (left) enjoyed many of his favorite outdoor activities. He loved to camp and hike in the mountains around his home.

Dick also had fun with his mother's father. Grandfather Dickey cooked for the workers on the Union Pacific Railroad. Young Dick spent vacations with his grandfather in a railroad car that followed the work crews.

Dick enjoyed his childhood in Lincoln, but it would not be his permanent home. When he was thirteen, the U.S. Department of Agriculture transferred his father to Casper, Wyoming. The family packed up, said good-bye to friends and relatives, and moved.

Casper was a great place for a boy who loved the outdoors. Mountains surround the city, and many streams flow nearby. Dick could fish in the streams and he could hike and camp in the mountains.

In 1955 Dick entered Natrona County High School. This was the same school where the people of Casper gathered to greet him during the 2000 election. Dick was an excellent student and got good grades. He was also very popular and a natural leader. In his senior year, he became president of his class.

Dick did not give up his love of sports, however. Stocky and well built, the teenager was a natural for football. He played halfback. He became cocaptain and then captain of the school team. Friends said that he might have seemed slow, but he was tough. When he tackled a player, the player knew it. Dick's mother was very proud of her son. She kept a scrapbook of clippings about his football days.

Dick, number 16, poses with his high school football teammates. Known as a tough player, he sometimes got injured, as the bandage on his hand shows.

While at Natrona, Dick met Lynne Anne Vincent. Lynne was helping out in the school office. Often Dick stopped by the office. Lynne and Dick hit it off. Soon they became high-school sweethearts.

Like Dick, Lynne was an excellent student and very popular. She was a champion baton twirler and leader of the baton squad. She was also homecoming queen. Dick was the king.

Dick and his high-school sweetheart, Lynne Vincent, attend their senior prom.

Dick and Lynne liked to go to dances and movies together. Although he was fun to be with, Dick had a serious side. Lynne remembers that other teens liked to drive their cars around town. They would go from "one root beer stand to another," she said. But not Dick. He wasn't interested in that. He liked reading, being outdoors, and playing sports better.

Friends remember that adults as well as teens liked Dick a lot. They felt he was very responsible. Often parents would let their sons go out in the evening if Dick was with them. They could count on Dick to keep things from getting rowdy.

Dick kept very busy studying, playing football, and dating Lynne. But he also worked. He had jobs delivering newspapers and working in a restaurant.

Off to College

IN 1959, DICK GRADUATED FROM HIGH SCHOOL. He got a scholarship to go to Yale University, a prestigious school in New Haven, Connecticut. But Dick did not do well at Yale and he lost his scholarship. A friend remembers that Dick "drank and got bad grades. . . . He was a big partier. A lot of beer." He stayed only a year and a half and then dropped out.

Dick later admitted that at the time he "wasn't interested in school. . . . I was more interested in going to

14

work. . . .," he said. "I never buckled down." Dick also said he did not like living in the East.

Dick had really missed the West. Westerners are known for minding their own business. Most like openness and plain speaking. The less someone talks, the better. Dick is like that. He has said, "I don't talk a lot about personal matters. That's the way I grew up, that's part of my western heritage, that's the way we are in Wyoming."

In 1962, Dick returned to Casper. He was not sure what his future would be. For a while he worked for a utility company. He laid down power lines in Wyoming for $2 an hour. The job didn't offer much of a future. He seemed to be drifting. He even got into trouble a couple of times. He was charged twice with drinking while driving. Finally, Dick realized he had to change his life. He was also thinking about Lynne. She had gone on to Colorado College in Colorado Springs. Dick knew he wanted to marry her someday. He also knew that "Lynne wasn't going to marry a [worker] for the county. I had to go make something of myself if I was going to [complete] the relationship. . . ."

In 1963, at the age of twenty-two, Dick Cheney decided to go back to college. This time he chose the University of Wyoming in Laramie. It was a western college where he could feel comfortable.

Once Cheney had made up his mind to get a college degree, he buckled down. He decided to study political

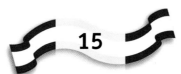

Dick's junior yearbook photo at the University of Wyoming. Once Dick got serious about his education, he worked hard at his studies.

science, the study of government and how it works. According to friends, Cheney loved politics. One friend remembers that in 1964 he and Cheney had heated arguments about that year's presidential election. Dick Cheney also loved history—especially military history.

In just three years, Dick Cheney had earned two degrees—a bachelor's and a master's degree. He greatly

impressed his professors. He also impressed Lynne Vincent. Even before he got his degrees, she had agreed to marry him—in August 1964. At the time, she was just finishing her master's degree at the University of Colorado in Boulder.

Like many other students, Dick Cheney got his first real taste of politics while still in college. He took a job as an intern at the Wyoming state legislature. A legislature is a group of people who make laws. People who serve in a legislature are called lawmakers, legislators, or representatives. An intern works for people in a particular field and learns what those people do. Dick Cheney learned how politics and government work.

Being both a student and an intern was not easy. Cheney spent long hours doing both. Once committed, however, he did not shirk his responsibilities.

Dick Cheney had other responsibilities as well. In 1966 the Cheney's had their first child—a baby girl. They named her Elizabeth. The next year they moved to Madison, Wisconsin. Both were going to study for their Ph.D. degrees at the University of Wisconsin.

A New Career

WHY DID DICK CHENEY WANT ANOTHER DEGREE? He thought he would become a teacher. But politics still attracted him. While studying, he took a job working for Wiscon-

sin's Republican governor. Unlike his parents, who were Democrats, Dick had joined the Republican Party. One thing led to another. Then, in 1968, he accepted a job working for U.S. Congressman William Steiger. Steiger was also a Republican.

Working for a congressman meant moving to Washington, D.C., the home of the U.S. Congress. So Cheney gave up his studies. But he did not mind. At twenty-seven, Dick Cheney knew what his future career would be. He was on his way to a life in public service. To be in public service means to work for, or serve, the public. Politicians are public servants. So are other government workers such as policemen, firemen, and teachers.

Dick Cheney soon learned how Congress operated. He also showed he could work well with others, even with Democrats. His boss gave him high marks. Such praise was sure to gain attention in Washington. Government leaders were always looking for bright young people to serve as aides. In 1969, Cheney became a special assistant to Donald Rumsfeld, head of an important government agency, the OEO.

Just the year before, the Cheney's second daughter, Mary Claire, was born. Lynne Cheney was hoping to get a teaching job in Washington. In the meantime, she began writing articles for magazines. Being a writer worked out well. She could work at home while raising her two little girls.

Her husband, however, could not spend much time at home. He was very busy working at the OEO. Dick Cheney greatly impressed his boss, and the two formed a close friendship. Rumsfeld took notice when Cheney wrote a twelve-page memo telling how to improve the agency.

From 1970 to 1974, Dick Cheney's boss served in various government jobs. One of them was working in the White House as President Gerald Ford's chief of staff. Cheney went with Rumsfeld from post to post, and Rumsfeld relied on him a lot. When the older man was away, Cheney often filled in for him in meetings with the president. Rumsfeld could be abrupt with people. Sometimes Cheney was called on to smooth things over.

Dick Cheney was learning the ins and outs of politics and how to get things done. Rumsfeld said, "Dick has natural good judgment and instincts. . . . he's very easy for people to get along with." In Washington, getting along with people is very important.

A Big Break

IN 1975, DICK CHENEY GOT THE BIGGEST BREAK SO FAR in his career. His boss became secretary of defense and Cheney took over the job as President Ford's chief of staff. At the age of thirty-four, he was the youngest chief of staff to ever serve a president.

At a 1975 White House press conference,
Donald Rumsfield (right) announces that Dick Cheney
(left) will be President Ford's new chief of staff.

A chief of staff has heavy responsibilities. Cheney
supervised the nearly five hundred people who worked
in the White House. He checked papers and documents
going to the president. He arranged the president's
schedule.

Always on the go, Dick and a waving President Ford make
their way toward Air Force One, the president's personal plane.
As chief of staff, Dick was a key adviser to Ford.

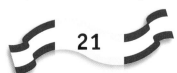

Like most White House workers, Dick Cheney kept up a hectic pace. Most of the time, he worked fifteen hours a day. But he kept what others have called his "laid-back" style. As chief of staff he could have been driven around in a government limousine. But he refused. He drove to and from his home in the suburbs of Washington in an old, beat-up Volkswagen.

Having a laid-back style didn't stop Cheney from speaking his mind. In 1975, President Ford was preparing to run for a second term. He wanted the backing of prominent Republicans, especially Senator Barry Goldwater of Arizona. It seemed to Cheney that Ford was not pushing Goldwater hard enough for a decision. So the chief of staff sent the president a memo. Very bluntly he told him to get tough.

One of Dick Cheney's most important jobs as chief of staff was recommending people for government jobs. In 1975, President Ford needed a new director of the Central Intelligence Agency. The agency collects information about foreign governments. Often this information is top secret. The president wanted George Bush Senior, who was then chairman of the Republican National Committee. George Bush Senior is the father of George W. Bush. Other advisers didn't want George Bush Senior, but Dick Cheney did.

The president listened to Cheney. He gave George Bush Senior the job. This was the first time Cheney had

dealings with the Bush family. But it would not be the last. The Bushes never forgot that Cheney had helped George Bush Senior.

Cheney's political career seemed to be on the rise. But in 1976, President Ford lost reelection. Democrat Jimmy Carter came into the White House. Dick Cheney was out of a job.

The Congressman from Wyoming

DICK CHENEY KNEW THAT HE WANTED TO STAY in public service. Says a friend, "[Dick Cheney] had politics in his blood." But what should he do now? Cheney decided to run for Congress in the next election. Wyoming is the least populated of the fifty states. So it sends just one representative to Washington. Dick wanted to be that representative.

Wyoming is heavily Republican. Dick seemed to be a sure winner. He was a loyal Republican. He had experience in government. And he was popular. He began to prepare his campaign. Then, one night in June 1978, calamity struck. Dick and Lynne Cheney were staying at the house of a friend, Joseph Meyer, in Cheyenne. Cheney suddenly felt a tingling in his left arm. Alarmed, his wife and friend rushed him to the hospi-

Dick Cheney easily won election
as Wyoming's only U.S. congressman.

tal. They were horrified to learn that he had suffered a mild heart attack.

Lynne Cheney was very upset. How would this affect the family? Would her husband have to give up politics? What would become of their two little girls? But Cheney was calm. Meyer recalls that when Cheney got back from the hospital, the family met together and talked. Dick Cheney convinced them that his heart attack should not spoil their plans. "They picked up the reins of the campaign and got on with things," says Meyer. Cheney did make one change though. He had been a three-pack-a-day smoker. Smoking is hard on your heart. Cheney gave up smoking.

Dick Cheney won election easily. He got nearly 60 percent of the vote. Now he was going back to Washington.

As the congressman from Wyoming, one of Cheney's major jobs was to look out for the needs of his state. Wyoming has many natural resources such as water and forests. He helped protect them.

One time, during a water shortage, some other western congressmen asked to borrow Wyoming's share of Colorado River water. "No way," Cheney said. "Once they get it, we'll never get it back. That's how things work."

Cheney did know how "things worked." Although he generally disagreed with the Democrats on issues, he

was practical. He knew he had to work with Democrats to get something done. And Democratic congressmen respected and liked him. One, Lee Hamilton, said of Cheney: ". . . Dick has always been a person you can take ideas to and see how he reacts to them. You can confide in him."

Cheney's fellow Republicans saw him as a "go-along, get-along guy." They gave him important posts on several committees. Then, in 1988, they elected him their "whip." Each party in Congress has a whip. The whip is the number two leadership spot for each party. The whip's job is to persuade congresspersons of his party to stick together—to support the party's policies and vote with the party leadership.

Although many in Congress praised Dick Cheney, others criticized him. A few thought that he had a mean side. In politics, one always has both supporters and critics. Those in the opposing party tend to be the critics. This is only natural as each party has its own ideas about what is best for the country.

The people of Wyoming were happy with the job Dick Cheney did in Congress. They elected him to Congress five times. He probably would have been elected many more times, but a higher position was about to come his way.

Secretary of Defense

IN 1988, GEORGE BUSH SENIOR WAS ELECTED U.S. president. He took office in early 1989. President Bush needed someone to head the Department of Defense (DoD). The DoD is in charge of the military forces that protect our country. President Bush wanted Dick

President George Bush (center) with top advisers Dick Cheney (left), General Colin Powell (right front), Vice President Dan Quayle (center rear), and others talk to reporters about the progress of the Gulf War.

Cheney for the post of secretary of defense. George Bush had not forgotten that Cheney had supported him years before. And the president also knew that Dick Cheney was a team player. A team player is someone who works well with a group—like players on a sports team.

Opponents objected to Cheney's appointment as secretary of defense. He had no military experience, they said. Critics also questioned Cheney's health. Only the year before, he had another heart attack—his third. It required surgery. He assured everyone he was healthy. He pointed out that he had gone back to work in Congress after only three weeks. He also pointed out that he was able to go skiing with his family at Christmastime. Could a sick person ski? He got the job.

As secretary of defense, Cheney directed and controlled all the nation's military forces. Even generals had to do what he said. He was a pretty tough boss. He demanded hard work and loyalty. He did not like those who wanted glory for themselves. At one point, he fired a general who gave military information to reporters.

At the same time, Cheney worked behind the scenes. Some said he was even secretive. He would meet with the president and other heads of government to discuss policies. But he would rarely tell his staff or reporters what had been discussed. He kept such a low profile that his Secret Service guards gave him the code name "Back-

seat." Others called him "Deadpan Dick." (The Secret Service provides guards for all high government officials.)

War in the Middle East

BUT DICK CHENEY WAS SOON TO TAKE THE FRONT SEAT. It all started in 1990. That August the nation of Iraq invaded and took over its neighbor Kuwait. Iraq's dictator, Saddam Hussein, claimed that Kuwait was really part of his territory. Saddam's invasion of Kuwait also threatened another Middle Eastern nation, the kingdom of Saudi Arabia.

The United States was alarmed. Saudi Arabia was a friend. It was also an oil-rich nation. The United States bought a lot of oil from Saudi Arabia. President Bush and Dick Cheney jumped into action right away. They offered to send fighter planes to protect Saudi Arabia. They also began plans to send thousands of troops and military equipment to that nation. But Saudi Arabia's king, Fahd, hesitated. He did not like the idea of having so many foreign soldiers in his country. It was up to Cheney to persuade him.

Dick Cheney flew to Saudi Arabia and met King Fahd and his advisors. He pointed out that large numbers of troops were necessary to protect Saudi Arabia.

Dick Cheney meets with a Saudi Arabian
general during the Gulf War.

He also said that the troops would only stay as long as
the king wanted them. Cheney's arguments were effec-
tive. In the end the king agreed.

Before leaving Saudi Arabia, Cheney put on his jeans
and cowboy boots. Then he inspected Air Force soldiers
already stationed in the country. He told them to prepare
for a war with Iraq. He also told them that the outcome
would be victory.

Dick Cheney looks over maps with military
commanders in Saudi Arabia and gets a
"briefing" explaining how the war is going.

The United States sent many troops and weapons into the region. The troops battled Saddam Hussein's soldiers in Kuwait with tanks and missiles. Meanwhile, the U.S. Air Force bombed targets inside Iraq itself. Soon Saddam Hussein's troops were driven from Kuwait. Kuwait and Saudi Arabia were safe.

The Gulf War, as the battle was called, lasted only a few weeks. Cheney had called for a massive air and ground war. His strategy worked. The military might of Iraq had crumbled. Along with his military chief of staff, General Colin Powell, Dick Cheney was now truly famous.

Time to Relax

THROUGHOUT CHENEY'S YEARS IN WASHINGTON, he worked very hard. Often he worked long into the night and on weekends. Lynne Cheney was busy, too, writing articles and making speeches about her favorite cause—education. Even with their important responsibilities, the couple still tried to take time off in the summers with their daughters. Cheney still loved the outdoors. The family's favorite vacations were backpacking and fishing trips. They also liked skiing and horseback riding. Their favorite vacation spots were in the Rocky Mountains.

Even in Washington, Cheney had fishing on his mind. He often stopped in sporting goods stores to buy

The Cheneys take every opportunity to enjoy
the outdoors. Here Dick and Lynne go horseback
riding with their granddaughter

fishing gear. Even so, when he spent a week fishing in the Wind River Mountains, he borrowed President Bush's prized fishing rod. After the girls grew up and left home, the couple continued to vacation out west.

While Cheney served as Defense Secretary, he and his wife lived in McLean, Virginia. They often attended parties there and in Washington. People noticed that Cheney—always the westerner—usually turned up in his cowboy boots.

Five Years in Business

IT LOOKED AS IF DICK CHENEY'S FUTURE in public service was set. But President Bush was defeated in the 1992 election. Democrat Bill Clinton took over the White House. Once again, Dick Cheney was out of politics.

For a time, Cheney considered running for president in the next election. He raised some money and talked it over with his wife and his supporters. They advised him against it. Campaigning is hard, they said. It is practically a twenty-four-hour job. He would have no time with his family. In the end, Cheney took his friends' advice.

The Cheneys returned to their second home in Jackson, Wyoming. Here they could relax, and Cheney had time to fish. He had no idea that fishing would lead to a new career in business.

On a salmon-fishing trip to Canada, Cheney met some businessmen who were impressed with his work as secretary of defense. One of the men offered Cheney a job as the head of his company, Halliburton, Inc. The company provides construction and oil drilling services

Dick Cheney shows off a new fishing rod. Whether traveling on business or for pleasure, he often stops at stores to stock up on fishing equipment.

to large oil companies. Cheney accepted the job. In 1995 the Cheneys moved to Dallas, Texas, where the company was based.

Dick Cheney had no experience in the oil business. But he did have connections with oil-producing companies in the Middle East. As head of Halliburton, Cheney would deal with many of the same people he had known when he was secretary of defense. His connections could throw a lot of business to Halliburton. Cheney also knew many people with influence in the government. He could help Halliburton get contracts to do work for the government.

Cheney spent five years at Halliburton. Critics say he wasn't as good in business as he was in government. They say he let others take over too many tasks he should have done. Also, Halliburton had money problems when Cheney was in charge. Others point out that the company grew under Cheney's leadership and made millions of dollars.

As head of Halliburton, Dick Cheney was out of the public spotlight. That was about to change.

On the Campaign Trail

George W. Bush, son of the former president and now governor of Texas, decided to run for president in the 2000 election. He needed a running mate to be vice

president. George W., a Republican, asked Dick Cheney to help him find someone. Then on July 25, 2000, George W. made a surprise announcement. He had found someone himself—Dick Cheney. Who could be better? Dick was a family friend. He was loyal and he

During Campaign 2000, Dick Cheney and
George W. Bush sometimes traveled by train.
Here, they wave to onlookers outside Battle Creek, Michigan.

was a team player. The Bush family places great value on these traits. Cheney also had years of experience in government. George W.'s political experience was only as governor of Texas.

Republicans instantly praised the selection. Democrats attacked it. They pointed out that Dick Cheney had voted against many social programs when he was in Congress. Social programs are designed to help people with jobs, health care, and education.

A further problem concerned Cheney's health. He had had three heart attacks in twenty-two years. He watched his diet, took medicine, and exercised. His doctors said he was fine. Still, people wondered if this fifty-nine-year-old, rather plump man was healthy enough to run.

The campaign would be a tough one. Republicans and Democrats strongly disagreed on many policies. Republicans wanted to give people a huge tax cut. Democrats said that such a big cut would mainly favor the wealthy. Republicans promised to give some money to parents who could not afford to send their children to private schools. Democrats replied that would hurt public schools by taking money away from them. Republicans had a plan to help the elderly pay less for prescription medicine. Democrats said that the plan would only help a few elderly people. Democrats promised that their plan would help all senior citizens.

Dick Cheney firmly believed in the ideas of the Republican Party. He and other Republicans believed that the government was too big and spent too much money. When Dick was in Congress, he had voted against many programs that would help improve people's education and health care. He said these programs cost too much. But he always supported big tax cuts and spending money on the military.

As Cheney campaigned around the West and Midwest, he made speeches that expressed his and the Republican Party's ideas. He told people that the military forces were weak. Republicans would make the military strong again, he said. He talked about how Republicans would reform, or make better, health care and education. He also called for big tax cuts.

Dick Cheney's campaign was a family affair. His daughter Elizabeth Cheney Perry, who is a lawyer, helped him with his speeches. His other daughter, Mary, helped organize things. She made sure he was on time for his speeches and that he didn't make long speeches. One of Cheney's little granddaughters even campaigned.

Dick Cheney is not the usual kind of politician. He isn't a very exciting speaker. He usually stands still and hardly ever raises his voice. He tends to keep his hands in his pockets. He seemed uncomfortable going into crowds and shaking hands. His wife, Lynne, once

For the Cheneys, campaigning is a family affair.
Here Dick and Lynne are joined by their granddaughter
Kate Perry at a gathering in Jackson Hole, Wyoming.

described Dick as ". . .an unusual politician, not a back-slapping kind of guy."

Lynne Cheney on the other hand is very good at campaigning. It was up to her to "warm up" crowds at rallies. She often introduced her husband as a "father and fisherman." She usually told some stories about his childhood. She chatted with people in the crowd. She also strongly criticized her husband's Democrat opponents, Vice President Al Gore and Senator Joseph Lieberman of Connecticut. Dick Cheney hardly ever mentioned their names.

As the campaign went on, Cheney lightened up a little. He told some jokes. He tried not to be too stiff. But he was more at ease talking to his supporters at football games, which he loves to attend. At a game in Ann Arbor, Michigan, he had a picnic with fans in the parking lot. After he spoke about his ideas, he chatted about his favorite hobby—fishing.

The Forty-Sixth Vice President

By November 6, 2000, the campaigning was over. As Americans cast their votes on election day, November 7, the results seesawed back and forth. First it seemed that Governor Bush and Dick Cheney were ahead. Then, Democrats Al Gore and Joe Lieberman moved up. It began to look as if the voters were evenly divided between the two parties.

Before taking office, a vice president must take
an oath swearing that he will faithfully serve the
United States. Here Dick rests his left hand on a Bible
held by daughter Elizabeth as he takes the oath.

Around 9 P.M. television commentators announced
that Gore and Lieberman had won the vote in Florida.
Democrats went wild. Florida was a key state. Winning
it would carry Al Gore over the top. Then, a short time

later, reporters on television stunned Americans. They had made a mistake. Gore had not won Florida after all. George W. Bush had. Now Republicans went wild.

The events that followed were among the strangest in America's history. Governor Bush was prepared to claim victory. He asked Cheney to go to Washington to begin getting things ready for the change of government. But before Cheney could even begin, Democrats challenged the election results. They said that the votes in Florida had not been counted properly. They wanted these votes to be recounted. Both sides went to court to try and settle the conflict. For more than a month, Americans waited to find out who would be president and vice president.

While the parties were fighting it out, Dick Cheney had another heart attack. Doctors said it was mild. Dick was out of the hospital in three days. He said he felt fine and was ready to go on with his duties.

Finally, on December 12, the conflict was decided by the U.S. Supreme Court, the highest court in the land. The Court decided that no more votes should be recounted. It ruled that George W. Bush should be the next president of the United States. That meant Dick Cheney would be the nation's forty-sixth vice president— and the first vice president of America's new millennium.

How did folks in Casper feel? Most were proud, especially those who came out one July morning in 2000 to greet their hometown hero.

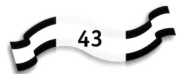

How important is the job of vice president? Very!

The vice president has the number two spot in the U.S. government. He or she is next in line to become president if anything happens to the president. So the vice president must always be prepared to become president.

The vice president is also president of the U.S. Senate. In that job, the vice president calls the Senate to order and enforces Senate rules. If there is a tie vote in the Senate, the Vice President casts the vote that breaks the tie.

Often the vice president helps the president. Sometimes he makes speeches and attends public gatherings in place of the president.

Some vice presidents have stayed in the background and have had very little power. Others have been in the public eye. For example, former Vice President Al Gore had many important duties. He was in charge of programs dealing with the environment, energy, and technology.

As vice president, Dick Cheney will also be active. He actually has more experience in government than President Bush. He will help President Bush select advisers. He will sit in on important meetings. He will be a major adviser to the president.

IMPORTANT DATES

1941	Dick Cheney is born on January 30 in Lincoln, Nebraska.
1959	Graduates from high school and enters Yale University.
1962	Drops out of Yale and works as lineman.
1963	Resumes education at University of Wyoming.
1964	Marries Lynne Ann Vincent in August.
1965	Serves as an intern in the Wyoming State Legislature and graduates from University of Wyoming.
1966	Receives M.A. degree from University of Wyoming and has a daughter, Elizabeth
1967	Studies for Ph.D. degree at University of Wisconsin and works for Wisconsin's governor.
1968	Gets job with Wisconsin Congressman William Steiger and moves to Washington D.C. Has another daughter, Mary.
1969	Accepts job at OEO, a government agency,
1970–1974	Works at various government jobs and briefly in business.
1975	Becomes President Gerald Ford's chief of staff.
1978	Wins election as U.S. congressman from Wyoming.
1979–1989	Serves in U.S.Congress.
1989	Becomes secretary of defense and serves three years.
1995	Joins Halliburton, Inc. and stays five years.
2000	Runs as the Republican candidate for the vice presidency.
2001	Inaugurated as forty-sixth U.S. vice president, January 20.

INDEX

Page numbers in *italics* refer to illustrations.